THIS PLANNER BELONGS TO:

_____

IF FOUND PLEASE CONTACT:

_____

_____

_____

CLIENT LIST

Client Name	Address	Contact Info

CLIENT LIST

Client Name	Address	Contact Info

OFF LEASH PARKS

Park Name	Location	Hours

OFF LEASH PARKS

Park Name	Location	Hours

DOG FRIENDLY PARKS

Park Name	Location	Hours

DOG FRIENDLY PARKS

Park Name	Location	Hours

DOGS

Breed	Name	Specific Needs

DOGS

Breed	Name	Specific Needs

Dog Walking Schedule
Date:

	Client	Pet Name:_____
6 am		TO DO
7		
8		
9		
10		
11		
12 pm		
1		
2		GOALS
3		
4		
5		
6		
7		
8		

NOTES:

IMPORTANT NOTES AND REMINDERS

Dog Walking Schedule

Date:

	Client	Pet Name:_____
6 am		TO DO
7		
8		
9		
10		
11		
12 pm		
1		
2		GOALS
3		
4		
5		
6		
7		
8		

NOTES:

IMPORTANT NOTES AND REMINDERS

Dog Walking Schedule
Date:

	Client	Pet Name:_____
6 am		TO DO
7		
8		
9		
10		
11		
12 pm		
1		
2		GOALS
3		
4		
5		
6		
7		
8		

NOTES:

IMPORTANT NOTES AND REMINDERS

Dog Walking Schedule

Date:

	Client	Pet Name:_____
6 am		TO DO
7		
8		
9		
10		
11		
12 pm		
1		
2		GOALS
3		
4		
5		
6		
7		
8		

NOTES:

IMPORTANT NOTES AND REMINDERS

Dog Walking Schedule

Date:

	Client		Pet Name:_____
6 am			TO DO
7			
8			
9			
10			
11			
12 pm			
1			
2			GOALS
3			
4			
5			
6			
7			
8			

NOTES:

IMPORTANT NOTES AND REMINDERS

Dog Walking Schedule

Date:

	Client	Pet Name:_____
6 am		TO DO
7		
8		
9		
10		
11		
12 pm		
1		
2		GOALS
3		
4		
5		
6		
7		
8		

NOTES:

IMPORTANT NOTES AND REMINDERS

Dog Walking Schedule
Date:

	Client	Pet Name:_____
6 am		TO DO
7		
8		
9		
10		
11		
12 pm		
1		
2		GOALS
3		
4		
5		
6		
7		
8		

NOTES:

IMPORTANT NOTES AND REMINDERS

Dog Walking Schedule
Date:

	Client	Pet Name:_____
6 am		TO DO
7		
8		
9		
10		
11		
12 pm		
1		
2		GOALS
3		
4		
5		
6		
7		
8		

NOTES:

IMPORTANT NOTES AND REMINDERS

Dog Walking Schedule

Date:

	Client	Pet Name:_____
6 am		TO DO
7		
8		
9		
10		
11		
12 pm		
1		
2		GOALS
3		
4		
5		
6		
7		
8		

NOTES:

IMPORTANT NOTES AND REMINDERS

Dog Walking Schedule

Date:

Client		Pet Name:_____
6 am		TO DO
7		_____
8		_____
9		_____
10		_____
11		_____
12 pm		
1		
2		GOALS
3		_____
4		_____
5		_____
6		_____
7		_____
8		_____

NOTES:

IMPORTANT NOTES AND REMINDERS

Dog Walking Schedule

Date:

	Client	Pet Name:_____
6 am		TO DO
7		
8		
9		
10		
11		
12 pm		
1		
2		GOALS
3		
4		
5		
6		
7		
8		

NOTES:

IMPORTANT NOTES AND REMINDERS

Dog Walking Schedule
Date:

	Client	Pet Name:_____
6 am		TO DO
7		
8		
9		
10		
11		
12 pm		
1		
2		GOALS
3		
4		
5		
6		
7		
8		

NOTES:

IMPORTANT NOTES AND REMINDERS

Dog Walking Schedule

Date:

	Client	Pet Name:_____
6 am		TO DO
7		
8		
9		
10		
11		
12 pm		
1		
2		GOALS
3		
4		
5		
6		
7		
8		

NOTES:

IMPORTANT NOTES AND REMINDERS

Dog Walking Schedule

Date:

	Client	Pet Name:_____
6 am		TO DO
7		
8		
9		
10		
11		
12 pm		
1		
2		GOALS
3		
4		
5		
6		
7		
8		

NOTES:

IMPORTANT NOTES AND REMINDERS

Dog Walking Schedule
Date:

	Client	Pet Name:_____
6 am		TO DO
7		
8		
9		
10		
11		
12 pm		
1		
2		GOALS
3		
4		
5		
6		
7		
8		

NOTES:

IMPORTANT NOTES AND REMINDERS

Dog Walking Schedule
Date:

	Client	Pet Name:_____
6 am		TO DO
7		
8		
9		
10		
11		
12 pm		
1		
2		GOALS
3		
4		
5		
6		
7		
8		

NOTES:

IMPORTANT NOTES AND REMINDERS

Dog Walking Schedule

Date:

	Client	Pet Name:_____
6 am		TO DO
7		
8		
9		
10		
11		
12 pm		
1		
2		GOALS
3		
4		
5		
6		
7		
8		

NOTES:

IMPORTANT NOTES AND REMINDERS

Dog Walking Schedule
Date:

	Client	Pet Name:_____
6 am		TO DO
7		
8		
9		
10		
11		
12 pm		
1		
2		GOALS
3		
4		
5		
6		
7		
8		

NOTES:

IMPORTANT NOTES AND REMINDERS

Dog Walking Schedule
Date:

	Client	Pet Name:_____
6 am		TO DO
7		_____
8		_____
9		_____
10		_____
11		_____
12 pm		
1		
2		GOALS
3		_____
4		_____
5		_____
6		_____
7		_____
8		_____

NOTES:

IMPORTANT NOTES AND REMINDERS

Dog Walking Schedule

Date:

	Client	Pet Name:_____
6 am		TO DO
7		
8		
9		
10		
11		
12 pm		
1		
2		GOALS
3		
4		
5		
6		
7		
8		

NOTES:

IMPORTANT NOTES AND REMINDERS

Dog Walking Schedule
Date:

	Client	Pet Name:_____
6 am		TO DO
7		
8		
9		
10		
11		
12 pm		
1		
2		GOALS
3		
4		
5		
6		
7		
8		

NOTES:

IMPORTANT NOTES AND REMINDERS

Dog Walking Schedule
Date:

	Client	Pet Name:_____
6 am		TO DO
7		
8		
9		
10		
11		
12 pm		
1		
2		GOALS
3		
4		
5		
6		
7		
8		

NOTES:

IMPORTANT NOTES AND REMINDERS

Dog Walking Schedule

Date:

	Client	Pet Name:_____
6 am		TO DO
7		
8		
9		
10		
11		
12 pm		
1		
2		GOALS
3		
4		
5		
6		
7		
8		

NOTES:

IMPORTANT NOTES AND REMINDERS

Dog Walking Schedule
Date:

	Client	Pet Name:_____
6 am		TO DO
7		
8		
9		
10		
11		
12 pm		
1		
2		GOALS
3		
4		
5		
6		
7		
8		

NOTES:

IMPORTANT NOTES AND REMINDERS

Dog Walking Schedule

Date:

	Client	Pet Name:_____
6 am		TO DO
7		
8		
9		
10		
11		
12 pm		
1		
2		GOALS
3		
4		
5		
6		
7		
8		

NOTES:

IMPORTANT NOTES AND REMINDERS

Dog Walking Schedule

Date:

	Client	Pet Name:_____
6 am		TO DO
7		
8		
9		
10		
11		
12 pm		
1		
2		GOALS
3		
4		
5		
6		
7		
8		

NOTES:

IMPORTANT NOTES AND REMINDERS

Dog Walking Schedule

Date:

	Client	Pet Name:_____
6 am		TO DO
7		
8		
9		
10		
11		
12 pm		
1		
2		GOALS
3		
4		
5		
6		
7		
8		

NOTES:

IMPORTANT NOTES AND REMINDERS

Dog Walking Schedule
Date:

	Client	Pet Name:_____
6 am		TO DO
7		
8		
9		
10		
11		
12 pm		
1		
2		GOALS
3		
4		
5		
6		
7		
8		

NOTES:

IMPORTANT NOTES AND REMINDERS

Dog Walking Schedule

Date:

	Client	Pet Name:_____
6 am		TO DO
7		
8		
9		
10		
11		
12 pm		
1		
2		GOALS
3		
4		
5		
6		
7		
8		

NOTES:

IMPORTANT NOTES AND REMINDERS

Dog Walking Schedule
Date:

	Client	Pet Name:_____
6 am		TO DO
7		
8		
9		
10		
11		
12 pm		
1		
2		GOALS
3		
4		
5		
6		
7		
8		

NOTES:

IMPORTANT NOTES AND REMINDERS

Dog Walking Schedule
Date:

	Client	Pet Name:_____
6 am		TO DO
7		
8		
9		
10		
11		
12 pm		
1		
2		GOALS
3		
4		
5		
6		
7		
8		

NOTES:

IMPORTANT NOTES AND REMINDERS

Dog Walking Schedule

Date:

	Client	Pet Name:_____
6 am		TO DO
7		
8		
9		
10		
11		
12 pm		
1		
2		GOALS
3		
4		
5		
6		
7		
8		

NOTES:

IMPORTANT NOTES AND REMINDERS

Dog Walking Schedule

Date:

	Client	Pet Name:_____
6 am		TO DO
7		
8		
9		
10		
11		
12 pm		
1		
2		GOALS
3		
4		
5		
6		
7		
8		

NOTES:

IMPORTANT NOTES AND REMINDERS

Dog Walking Schedule
Date:

	Client	Pet Name:_____
6 am		TO DO
7		
8		
9		
10		
11		
12 pm		
1		
2		GOALS
3		
4		
5		
6		
7		
8		

NOTES:

IMPORTANT NOTES AND REMINDERS

Dog Walking Schedule

Date:

	Client	Pet Name:_____
6 am		TO DO
7		
8		
9		
10		
11		
12 pm		
1		
2		GOALS
3		
4		
5		
6		
7		
8		

NOTES:

IMPORTANT NOTES AND REMINDERS

Dog Walking Schedule

Date:

	Client	Pet Name:_____
6 am		TO DO
7		
8		
9		
10		
11		
12 pm		
1		
2		GOALS
3		
4		
5		
6		
7		
8		

NOTES:

IMPORTANT NOTES AND REMINDERS

Dog Walking Schedule

Date:

	Client	Pet Name:_____
6 am		TO DO
7		
8		
9		
10		
11		
12 pm		
1		
2		GOALS
3		
4		
5		
6		
7		
8		

NOTES:

IMPORTANT NOTES AND REMINDERS

Dog Walking Schedule

Date:

	Client	Pet Name:_____
6 am		TO DO
7		
8		
9		
10		
11		
12 pm		
1		
2		GOALS
3		
4		
5		
6		
7		
8		

NOTES:

IMPORTANT NOTES AND REMINDERS

Dog Walking Schedule

Date:

	Client	Pet Name:_____
6 am		TO DO
7		
8		
9		
10		
11		
12 pm		
1		
2		GOALS
3		
4		
5		
6		
7		
8		

NOTES:

IMPORTANT NOTES AND REMINDERS

Dog Walking Schedule

Date:

	Client	Pet Name:_____
6 am		TO DO
7		
8		
9		
10		
11		
12 pm		
1		
2		GOALS
3		
4		
5		
6		
7		
8		

NOTES:

IMPORTANT NOTES AND REMINDERS

Dog Walking Schedule

Date:

	Client	Pet Name:_____
6 am		TO DO
7		
8		
9		
10		
11		
12 pm		
1		
2		GOALS
3		
4		
5		
6		
7		
8		

NOTES:

IMPORTANT NOTES AND REMINDERS

Dog Walking Schedule

Date:

	Client	Pet Name:_____
6 am		TO DO
7		
8		
9		
10		
11		
12 pm		
1		
2		GOALS
3		
4		
5		
6		
7		
8		

NOTES:

IMPORTANT NOTES AND REMINDERS

Dog Walking Schedule

Date:

	Client	Pet Name:_____
6 am		TO DO
7		
8		
9		
10		
11		
12 pm		
1		
2		GOALS
3		
4		
5		
6		
7		
8		

NOTES:

IMPORTANT NOTES AND REMINDERS

Dog Walking Schedule

Date:

	Client	Pet Name:_____
6 am		TO DO
7		
8		
9		
10		
11		
12 pm		
1		
2		GOALS
3		
4		
5		
6		
7		
8		

NOTES:

IMPORTANT NOTES AND REMINDERS

Dog Walking Schedule

Date:

	Client	Pet Name:_____
6 am		TO DO
7		
8		
9		
10		
11		
12 pm		
1		
2		GOALS
3		
4		
5		
6		
7		
8		

NOTES:

IMPORTANT NOTES AND REMINDERS

Dog Walking Schedule

Date:

	Client	Pet Name:_____
6 am		TO DO
7		
8		
9		
10		
11		
12 pm		
1		
2		GOALS
3		
4		
5		
6		
7		
8		

NOTES:

IMPORTANT NOTES AND REMINDERS

Dog Walking Schedule

Date:

	Client	Pet Name:_____
6 am		TO DO
7		
8		
9		
10		
11		
12 pm		
1		
2		GOALS
3		
4		
5		
6		
7		
8		

NOTES:

IMPORTANT NOTES AND REMINDERS

Dog Walking Schedule
Date:

	Client	Pet Name:_____
6 am		TO DO
7		
8		
9		
10		
11		
12 pm		
1		
2		GOALS
3		
4		
5		
6		
7		
8		

NOTES:

IMPORTANT NOTES AND REMINDERS

Dog Walking Schedule

Date:

	Client	Pet Name:_____
6 am		TO DO
7		
8		
9		
10		
11		
12 pm		
1		
2		GOALS
3		
4		
5		
6		
7		
8		

NOTES:

IMPORTANT NOTES AND REMINDERS

Dog Walking Schedule

Date:

	Client	Pet Name:_____
6 am		TO DO
7		
8		
9		
10		
11		
12 pm		
1		
2		GOALS
3		
4		
5		
6		
7		
8		

NOTES:

IMPORTANT NOTES AND REMINDERS

Dog Walking Schedule

Date:

	Client	Pet Name:_____
6 am		TO DO
7		
8		
9		
10		
11		
12 pm		
1		
2		GOALS
3		
4		
5		
6		
7		
8		

NOTES:

IMPORTANT NOTES AND REMINDERS